Wood and plastic

peg	cup	spoon	bottle	
door	bag	scales	bowl	lego	ruler

Label the pictures using words from the box.
Colour brown the things made of wood.
Colour blue the things made of plastic.
Draw a ring around the things that can be made of wood
or plastic.

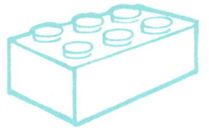

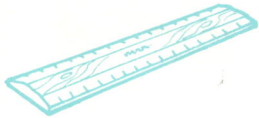

_____   _____   _____   _____

_____   _____   _____   _____

_____   _____   _____   _____

Now make a set of things made of wood and a set of things
made of plastic. Use things in the classroom. Draw the sets here.

things made of wood	things made of plastic

Metal and clay

Label the pictures using the words from the box.
Colour yellow the things made of metal.
Colour red the things made of clay.
Draw a ring around the things that can be made of metal or clay.

_____ _____ _____ _____

_____ _____ _____ _____

_____ _____ _____ _____

Now make a set of things made of metal and a set of things made of clay. Use things in the classroom. Draw the sets here.

things made of metal	things made of clay

4

Plastic

Collect some yoghurt pots. Helped by an adult, carefully put the pots in a pan of boiling water.
Watch what happens.
Draw a yoghurt pot.

before it went into hot water	after it came out of hot water

Write a sentence describing what happened to the pot in hot water.

_____

_____

Make a collage with your yoghurt pots.

Make a list of plastic things you have at home.

plastic in the kitchen	plastic in the bathroom	plastic in the bedroom

We have most plastic things in the _____ .

Metal

Find a metal grid and make a rubbing.
Walk around the outside of your school. What can you see made out of metal? Colour a space each time you see something.

											I saw
manhole cover											☐ manhole covers
grid											☐ grids
metal fence											☐ metal fences
metal gate											☐ metal gates
metal door handle											☐ metal door handles

What else did you see that is made of metal?
Complete the sentence. **I also saw metal** _____

_____

_____

Clean 9 nails with metal polish.
Collect 3 yoghurt pots and label them 1, 2, 3.

Put 3 nails in a drop of water and leave outside.

Put 3 nails in a dry pot and leave them inside for 2 weeks.

Put 3 nails in a dry pot and cover. Keep inside.

Leave the 3 pots for 2 weeks. Write what happened to the nails in each pot after 2 weeks.

Pot 1 _____

Pot 2 _____

Pot 3 _____

6

Clay

You will need 3 lumps of clay.
Make a ball with the 1st lump. Make a model with the 2nd lump.
Wrap the 3rd lump in some polythene.

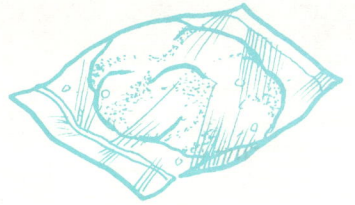

Leave your 1st and 2nd lumps of clay to dry. How long did they take to dry?

The 1st lump took ☐ days.   The 2nd lump took ☐ days.

Complete the sentence.

Now the clay looks _____ .

Ask an adult to help you to bake the clay in an oven. When the clay is baked, drop the ball on the floor. Now drop the 3rd lump of damp clay on the floor. Draw what happened.

dropped dry clay	dropped wet clay

Complete the sentences.

The dry clay _____ .

The wet clay _____ .

Paint your model.
Draw it.

Glass and paper

milk bottle	**box**	**glasses**	**wrapping paper**
card	**bowl**	**wine glass**	**tissues**
book	**marble**	**jam jar**	**toilet roll**

Label the pictures using the words from the box.
Colour the things made of glass red.
Colour the things made of paper blue.

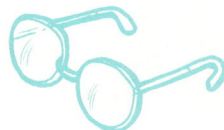

_____   _____   _____   _____

_____   _____   _____   _____

_____   _____   _____   _____

Now look around your classroom and make 2 sets.
Draw your sets here.

things made of glass	things made of paper

I found more things made of _____ .

8

Paper

Complete these sentences using words from the box.

Mum blows her nose with a _____ .

We dry our hands with a _____ .

Grandpa reads his _____ .

In the toilet we use _____ .

Mum puts _____ on the wall.

Our breakfast cereal comes in a _____ .

We buy milk from the shop in a _____ .

I write thank you letters on_____ .

Collect 6 pieces of coloured paper – blue, green, yellow, red, black and white.
Cut the 6 pieces of paper in half. Put one half of each colour on the window. Put the other half of each colour in a dark cupboard. Leave them for 5 days. Look at them each day. Compare the two halves of each colour. Record what happens.

| Colour | Order of fading | | Amount of fading |
	in light	in cupboard	
blue green yellow red black white			

_____ faded first.   _____ faded the most.

_____ did not fade at all.

9

Fabrics

Match the fabric to where it comes from.
Draw a blue ring round the man-made fabrics.
Draw a green ring round the natural fibres.

4

5

polyester

cotton

leather

6

nylon

rope

suede

2

Terylene

wool

1

linen

3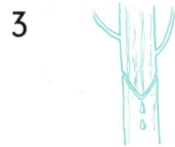

rubber

silk

Look at the numbered pictures.

Write the name of the fabrics in this crossword puzzle.

Look at the labels in your clothes. Write down the fabrics in the correct set.

man-made fabrics

natural fabrics

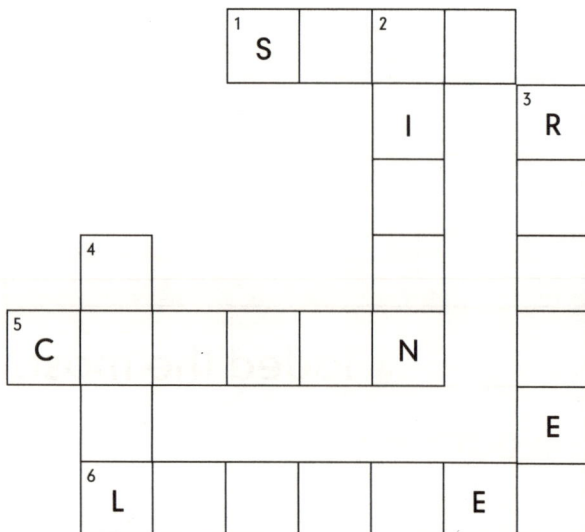

10

What are you wearing?

Look at the fabrics you and your friends are wearing. What are your clothes made of?
Complete the list of clothes you are wearing across the top of the chart.

Colour code:

cotton ⇨ blue

leather ⇨ red

wool ⇨ green

mixture ⇨ black

polyester ⇨ yellow

any other fabric ⇨ purple

Names	vest	pants	socks	shoes				
myself								

The fabric we wear most is _____ .

The fabric I wear most is _____ .

I like wearing _____ best.

Which fabric keeps you warm? _____

Which fabric helps you stay cool? _____

Which fabric is best for wearing in cold weather?

_____

11

Rough and smooth

Label the pictures using the words from the box.
Colour the rough things red.
Colour the smooth things blue.

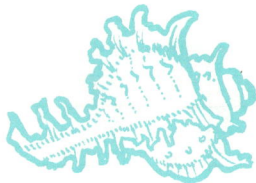

_____ _____ _____ _____

_____ _____ _____ _____

_____ _____ _____ _____

Look around the classroom. Make a collection of rough and smooth things. Write their names in the correct set.

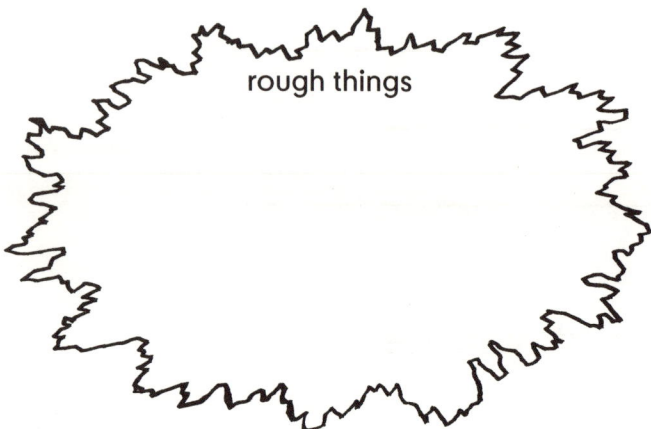

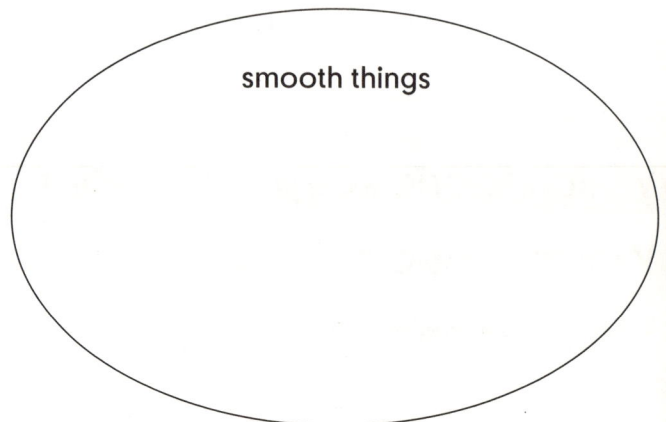

rough things

smooth things

12

Feel these objects

Colour a space to show whether the things are **rough** or **smooth**.
Write the materials they are made from.

Object		rough	smooth	material
rope				
bottle				
hot-water bottle				
spoon				
leaf				
tin				
matchbox				
pencil				
nail				
screw				
cork				

Answer yes or no.

Are all rough things made of the same material? _____

Are all smooth things made of the same material? _____

Some rough things are made of _____ .

Some smooth things are made of _____ .

13

Hard and soft

button   Plasticine   chicken   sock   medal   car
handkerchief   triangle   wool   button   key   ribbon

Label the pictures using the words from the box.
Colour all the soft things red.
Colour all the hard things blue.

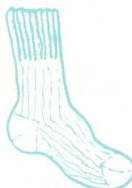

_____	_____	_____	_____
_____	_____	_____	_____
_____	_____	_____	_____

Look around the classroom. Make a collection of hard and soft things. Write their names in the correct set.

hard things

soft things

14

Feel these objects

Colour a space to show whether the things are **hard** or **soft**.
Write the material they are made from.

Object		hard	soft	material
cotton wool				
building block				
paper clip				
duster				
carrier bag				
feather				
rubber band				
book				
2p coin				
ruler				
teddy				
toy car				

Answer yes or no.

Are all hard things made of the same material? _____

Are all soft things made of the same material? _____

Some soft things are made of _____ .

Some hard things are made of _____ .

15

Which material?

Match the picture to the material.

wool
gwlan

glass
gwydr

metal
metal

paper
papur

fabric
fabrig

clay
clai

plastic
plastig

wood
pren

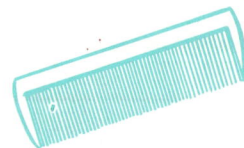

  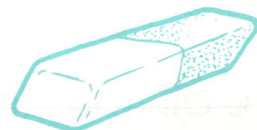

Colour rough things red and smooth things blue.

Write **h** under the hard things and **s** under the soft things.

16

Feeling

What does it feel like?
Colour the spaces to show what each object feels like.
Write down what it is made of.

Object		rough	smooth	hard	soft	material
rubber glove						
sack						
magnifying glass						
necklace						
pencil crayon						
polystyrene tile						
sandpaper						
sorting toy						
toothbrush						
silk flower						
envelope						
sieve						

Complete the sentences.

_____ is hard and smooth.

_____ is hard and rough.

_____ is rough and soft.

_____ is soft and smooth.

Transparent or opaque

Things you can see through are called **transparent**.
Things you cannot see through are called **opaque**.
Look at the following things. Colour a space to show whether they are transparent or opaque. Write down the material each one is made from.

Object		transparent	opaque	material
comic				
food bag				
medicine bottle				
egg shell				
net curtain				
pair of tights				
straw				
drinks can				
Cellophane paper				
Sellotape				
tree bark				
marble				

How many things are transparent? ☐ things are transparent

How many things are opaque? ☐ things are opaque

Things which only allow a little
light through are called **translucent**.
Can you find anything that is translucent?
Draw it here.

What sort of glass is used for a bathroom window and why?

18

Shiny or dull

Make a collection of things. Sort them into 2 sets: **shiny** or **dull**.
Draw them in the correct set. Write their names.

shiny things	dull things

Where do shiny things shine most, inside or outside?

_____

What are shiny things made of?

_____

_____

Find the shiny things and write their names.

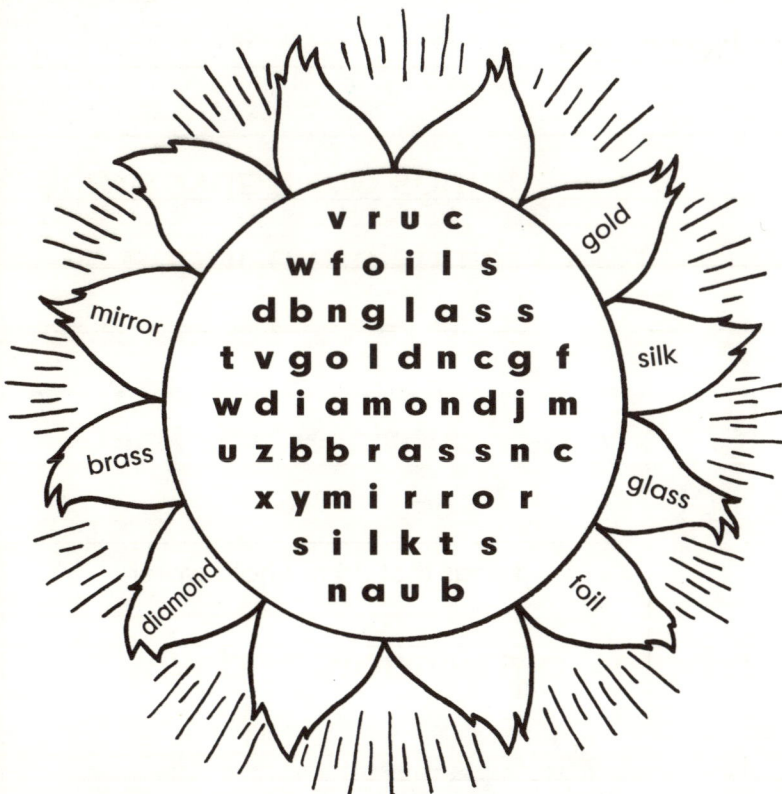

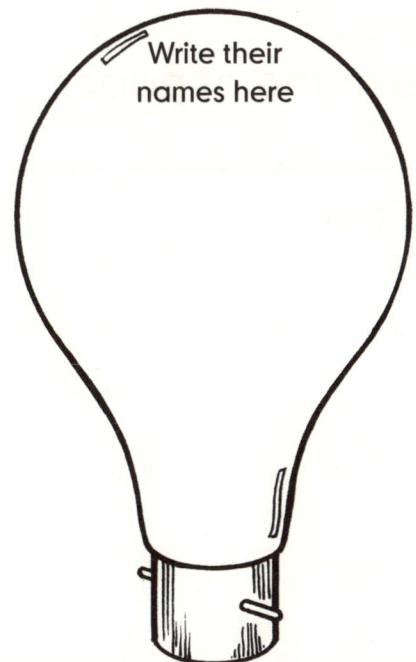

```
    v r u c
  w f o i l s
 d b n g l a s s
t v g o l d n c g f
w d i a m o n d j m
 u z b b r a s s n c
  x y m i r r o r
   s i l k t s
    n a u b
```

gold

mirror

silk

brass

glass

diamond

foil

Write their names here

Will it hold water?

Label the pictures using the words from the box.
Fill the containers with water. Watch what happens.
If the container will hold water, colour its picture blue.

_____   _____   _____   _____

_____   _____   _____   _____

_____   _____   _____   _____

Complete these sentences.

The basket did not hold water because _____

_____

Things made of paper_____

_____

The mitten _____

Look around the classroom and find some containers. Find out
whether they will hold water or not. Make 2 sets.

things that hold water	things that do not hold water

20

Is it waterproof?

When things are **waterproof** they do not let in water.

Collect the following materials and stretch them over a clear pot. Fasten with an elastic band. Pour a spoonful of water on top of each material.

What happens? If the water does not go through, the material is waterproof.

Colour the pot yellow if the material is waterproof.

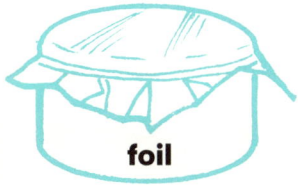
foil

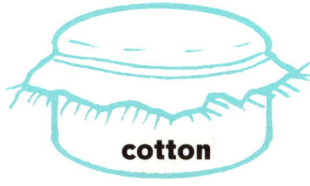
cotton

paper

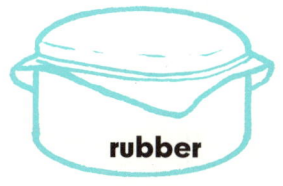
rubber

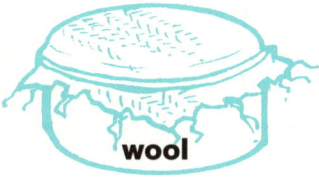
wool

plastic

newspaper

Cellophane

tights

paper kitchen towel

card

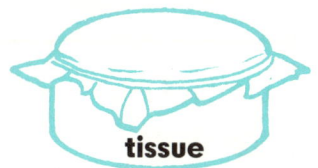
tissue

Answer these questions.

Which material is the most waterproof? _____

Why? _____

What happened to the card? _____

_____

Why are kitchen paper towels so useful?

_____

Which material would keep you driest in the rain?

_____

Soaking up water

Put these things into a bowl of water and then take them out.
Colour the correct space.

object	damp	wet but did not soak up the water	soaked up some of the water	soaked up a lot of the water
sponge				
tissue				
nail				
paper towel				
foil				
hand towel				
face cloth				
plastic bag				
paper				
wood				
wool				

Which material soaked up water immediately?

The _____ soaked up the water immediately.

Our food and water

Water is found in many things.
Add cold water to these foods and stir with a spoon.
Write about what happens.
Do the same again but this time add warm water.

Foods	cold water	warm water
sugar		
vinegar		
salt		
powdered milk		

Find these foods. The label will tell you if the food contains water. Tick in the box if they contain water.

☐ baked beans   ☐ peas   ☐ sauce   ☐ jam   ☐ soup   ☐ yoghurt

Collect as many food labels as you can and make 2 sets:
1. Foods containing water.   2. Foods without water.

Our senses and water

Sense	Things to do	Write what you think about each test.
Taste	Drink some cold water. Drink some warm water.	I think _____ _____ _____ _____
Touch	Feel cold water. Feel warm water. Feel dripping water. Feel pouring water.	I think _____ _____ _____ _____
Smell	Smell cold water. Smell hot water.	I think _____ _____ _____ _____
Sight	Look at a glass of water. Stand a straw in the water.	I think _____ _____ _____ _____
Hearing	Listen to dripping water. Listen to pouring water.	I think _____ _____ _____ _____

Mixing with water

Pour cold water from a jug on to these things.
Watch for a short time, then stir with a spoon.
Write down what happens.
Now do the same with warm water.

Pour the water on	cold water	warm water
food colouring		
flour		
powder paint		
sugar		
orange squash		
salt		
sand		
honey		
jelly cubes		
oil paint		
ice cube		

Pouring and carrying water

Use the sink for this experiment.
Pour water from a jug into these containers.

Circle the pictures of the containers you could not pour water into without spilling.

mug

narrow vase

jam jar

mixing bowl

wine bottle

food tray

perfume bottle

drinks can

Fill these objects with water.
Try pouring water from them without spilling.

pop bottle

saucepan

milk pan

cup

glass

jug

milk bottle

teapot

What makes it easier to pour water?

A _____ makes it easier to pour water.

26

Can water change things?

sugar   vinegar   Plasticine   soil   sugar cube
salt   sand   jelly   clay

Label the pictures using the words from the box.
Add all these things one at a time to water and watch what happens.
If they disappear, they have dissolved. Write down what happens.

_____

_____

_____

_____

_____

_____

_____

_____

_____

Make 2 sets.

things which dissolve	things which do not dissolve

Did anything dissolve immediately? _____

Did anything take a long time to dissolve? _____

27

Floating and sinking

Get a bowl of water.
Put each object in the water, one at a time.
Does the object float or sink?

 a stone
_____

 a nail
_____

 a cork
_____

 a metal spoon
_____

 an apple
_____

 a ball
_____

 a piece of soap
_____

 a rubber band
_____

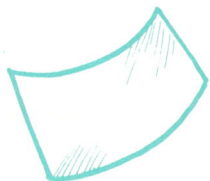 a piece of paper
_____

 a 1p coin
_____

 a plastic spoon
_____

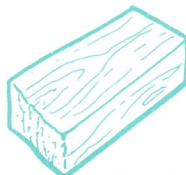 a piece of wood
_____

 a piece of foil
_____

 a plastic bag
_____

Floating and sinking

Get a bowl of water so that you can see if these objects float or sink.
Guess first, and write down whether you think they will float or sink. Then put each object into the water.
Put a ✓ if your guess is correct; a X if your guess is wrong.

floats   sinks

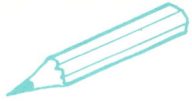 a pencil _____

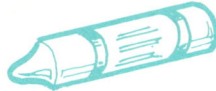 a crayon _____

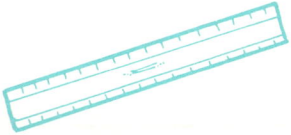 a ruler _____

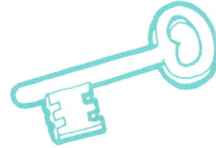 a key _____

 a tissue _____

a candle _____

 a sponge _____

a jam jar _____

 a straw _____

a milk bottle top _____

 a flat balloon _____

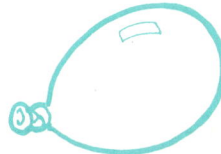 a blown up balloon _____

plastic   wood   metal   glass   rubber   wax   foil

What have you found out?

Which materials float?

Which materials sink?

Does anything float and then sink?

If so, what is it? _____ .

29

Cargo on a boat

floats   sinks

Make a Plasticine boat.
Float it in a bowl of water.
Find out how many nails it will carry before it sinks.
Write down whether the boat floats or sinks.

The empty boat _____ .

Put in 1 nail

The boat and 1 nail _____ .

Put in another nail

The boat and 2 nails _____ .

Add more nails one at a time. Count them.

The boat holds _____ nails before it sinks.

Now try the same thing with paper clips.

The boat and 1 paper clip _____

Put in another 3 paper clips

The boat and 4 paper clips _____

Carefully add more paper clips.

The boat holds _____ paper clips before it sinks

Will the boat float if it is full of water?

The boat _____ if it is full of water

Will the boat float if it is partly filled with water?

The boat _____ if it is partly filled with water